Under a Private Sky

Under a Private Sky

Poems by

Julie Adrian

© 2024 Julie Adrian. All rights reserved.
This material may not be reproduced in any form, published,
reprinted, recorded, performed, broadcast,
rewritten or redistributed without
the explicit permission of Julie Adrian.
All such actions are strictly prohibited by law.

Cover design by Shay Culligan
Cover art by Joey Gerdin

ISBN: 978-1-63980-500-6
Library of Congress Control Number: 2024935493

Kelsay Books
502 South 1040 East, A-119
American Fork, Utah 84003
Kelsaybooks.com

for Brooke and Everett

Contents

I.

Flight of a Peacock	15
Table Under a Tree	16
Human	17
The Great Lake Awoke	18
The Wind Eats Everything	19
Breathe Out a Lung	20
Under a Private Sky	21
Where am I in the world	22
The Hungry Wind	23
Reaching Across Constellations	24
The Owl	25
Good Hiding Spot	26
The Crinkling Trees	27
The Beautiful Wound	28
I wonder	29
Scribbles of a Child	30
I sometimes want to cry	31
Forest Tents	32
Looking Back in a Broken Mirror	33

II.

Hard Wake	37
Pond of Leaves	38
In Illness	39
Cold Spell	40
In the Dark	41
She saw the ends	43
Night Sleeps	44
Ears to the Sky	45
My Body Lay	46
Dream	47
Reason for Suffering	48
These little words	49

III.

Life Waiting on a Park Bench	53
Lost	54
A Bug	55
Foreign Accent	56
Stories	57
Mistaken Sisters of the Queen	58
What if perfection	59
High Horse	60
Outside Walls	61
The Empty Woman People Loved	62
Cough, Stand	63
Soulful Bearings	64
A Thousand Setting Suns	65
This Day	66

IV.

Wait for White	69
The Gray Day	70
Belief	71
The Top	72
I saw God	73
Hug the Tree	74
Gray Wolves	75
The Night Shivers	76
The Question You Have	77
Brush Wolf's Resolve	78
Wringing a Rag	79
The Great Spring Thaw	80
After her life washed away	81
The Small Bunny of the Wood	82
Fence of Foliage	83
Walking into Their World	84

V.

The Precious Table	87
Dead Life	88
The Slow Song	89
That day I looked away	90
Sinking House	91
Become the Person You Were	92
Courage	93
Early Morning	94
Whispers from Meaningful World	95
The Brush Wolf	96
From Treetops	97
Inner Land	98
Seals off the Coastline	99
His Favorite Armchair	100
The Day	101
The Ghost Herds	102
Fields of Quiet	103
Hopefully these short words	104
If She Doesn't Write	105
Heart to Hand	106

VI.

The Empty Fence	109
Feral Screech of Guinea Fowl	110
Blossoms by the Bed	111
Shells on Rotted Log	112
Every Child Has an Icon	113
Antique Cedar Table	115
A deaf world looks away	116
Bugs the Giant Steps On	117
Rain	118
The Bloody Feather	119

Fallen Trees   120
The Last Days of Summer   121
Fleeting Summer   122
Breath of Winter Forest   123
The Crisp Fall Morning   124
Show Yourself   125
Morning Glass   126
Textures of Beauty   127
In Winter   128
The Snow World   129
Hello, Stranger   130

VII.

Stories of Wind   133
Warm Secrets   134
The Clearing   135
World Child Created   136
The Black Boulder   137
Little stars still fall   138
The Trombone Player   139
Little Suns   140
The Children's Questions   141
A Day, an Adventure   142
The Maze Garden   143
The Child's Heart   144
Barbed-Wire Spools   145
The Most Human Among Us   146
On the North Shore   147
This Old World   148

I.

Flight of a Peacock

I saw a peacock among the fields,
perched on the crown of cottonwood,
supple branches oscillate,
hand waving in the wind.
High above the world, the tree is
his throne, the fruitful harvest
and jewels of bountiful trees below
his kingdom. His exotic plume,
quills of majestic turquoise eyes,
embroidered with metallic, virescent thread
for all the world to see.
But does this feather know flight?

It's like every great thing we do.
Its flight was born of sheer belief,
from the sight of sparrows with natural
torque spattering the wind at trees
and clouds without yield.
And eagles elegantly
floating at great heights who only fall up
with a string attached
to the sun.

Table Under a Tree

I lived at home outside in a cow pasture for
eighteen years. It was a table under an apple tree.
In hell, nothing is as it seems. In the house,
we had to sit in the corner, when we lived
our lives. We all made things out of nothing.
If something is absent, it can also be there.
The moon listened to the rain streaking
down my face. One day, I went out into
the world. It was full of what
the house wouldn't let on. I eaves-
dropped on music, inspiration, and
the reason for joy. Everything the
emptiness was afraid of filled the air.
I saw things without a shadow
living in the sun.

Human

Every summer, she cried like the wild sea
in the wind at her mother looking in the mirror,
hoping somebody would hear. She shouted,
you don't love me, which sounded like swear words
echoing in her ears. Hid in her mother's closet,
from a fiery dragon who said, there's no room
for you.

The echoes of a stranger's name turning into
television, she ran down the deer paths the hunters
shared, the hours which felt like days balancing
on a rope of midnight shoulder. Walked to the
graveyard of sleeping souls, stepping softly, so not
to wake precious porcelain sticks. Where father's
vessel would later lay to rest. What is this life?

The grief fell out in the moonlight. She headed back
through the cow pasture, sidestepping fresh
landmines. Came upon the table she had dragged
under the old apple tree the farmer saved,
bees swirling saccharine bouquets, it flowering
fungus, a friend who knew prison before it
deserved to see the sun. You are human, it said,
this is your earth too.

The Great Lake Awoke

The great lake woke in a rumpled mess.
A rogue wave tumbled into a trapped cove,
to wash picnickers and arks away in a sneeze,
those who mistakenly believe sand is land
and wouldn't come when it hears mother's call.

The water crashed rough on bows of boats,
and rocks of snarling wolves rising from bed.
Scaly crescents with gills of wet sky
slipping in the water didn't notice
any difference.

The lake's ancient reaching fingers clamber
around dry throats, pulling back land-
dwellers kicking, let me walk,
short a pair of gills.

The Wind Eats Everything

I peeked into her room,
to sniff out if she was day or night,
then sat down with her or ran away.
When I came looking for love, like children do,
waiting on the threshold with a blooming ear,
she gave what her mother gave her,
love that lay like a flat gray sky.
She had to be loved by the deer
she invited in and found out were wolves,
and by the wolves she already knew were wolves;
the unconditional, loving arms of the mother womb
didn't hold her close as a baby.

She tried to make herself feel better,
by asking about the meanest moments first.
Would spit barely missing my shoe,
for some reason or other, like the sun wasn't closer
or the wind was grainy that day.
The people who saw her from a distance loved her
because they already had a mother.
There was no one more like the world,
all the beauty and ugliness laid out shamelessly
on a smorgasbord it openly gulps down.

Like the wind she ate everything with her heart
and mind like the first day
in disbelief she was alive.

Breathe Out a Lung

You can't control the wolves' yipping
yonder in the clearing,
though you may know it well.
They snarl grow more vicious,
laughing into the night.
I hear the cries of bunnies
like the abandoned babies in baskets
floating down the river.

You do not need to know exactly
the shadow behind every evil face.
They always long to pull somebody in
to kick in the soul with a horse hoof
to take on a wound.

I am not responsible for their teeth,
the tribe, or the world's outcome.
You need to only play the role assigned to you
by God. I can breathe out a lung—

my portion is quiet and important,
to let the sweet texture of my voice rise,
the life growing inside that is told,
don't be so serious.

Under a Private Sky

We were raised by the wild field, running through,
our feet permanently stained with dirt.
We picked ticks off like flowers from fields,
tripping over bull snakes we saw not until the
last moment. We nailed together forts
from scraps of wood, a porcupine with metal quills
poking out, picking the spot out carefully
like a plot for a house.

We dug a deep pit to try to go to China
because Mom wouldn't take us on vacation,
garter snakes and frogs filling it up thinking
my brother's name was Joseph. Bulbs of fire
crossed the thirsty prairie by my sister's restless strike.
We waggled buckets full to the sound of sirens singing,
warning us if it happened again. Sledding down
around the thorn bush, we stumbled in face bloodied
from the bush to the loving dog's sandy lick.

We stayed up past midnight with a chorus of ideas
that would change the world, thinking
this would last forever. We knew simple things,
like you could be anywhere you wanted to be
without going and war was hell; other things
no one says, but children know. We thought
we knew everything but didn't know
warmth made children blossom.

Sunday morning trying if not to listen,
to think about God, staring at the ceiling
counting fake stars. We sang our name
proudly surfing in the bed of a rusty old truck,
going down our private road, to be home where
we lived mightily, where dream was our world,
living on a hilltop with trees holding hands
in a large braided wreath.

Where am I in the world and where did I come from?
I don't remember, partly, because birth is painful.
Partly, because I just don't remember.
It was long ago and new lives override
the poorer lives you lead. The full house is true
if the empty house is.

I need to know the world, to know
where I am. That's God's job.

The Hungry Wind

The gust wailed tired and hungry
last night. It wrapped our limbs
around us in love of true self.
It slipped rubber soles in the air,
plucked feathers off birds bare clad,
before they could outright caw,
banged doors clapping about life.

The wind easily uprooted tawdry
edifice off the earth, as hastily
as it was built—
it wasn't God's style anyways.

Then acted like it was nothing,
whistling Frank Sinatra
down an open country road
among undressed oak trees.

Reaching Across Constellations

Her mother love lay flat, without a
laughing wink in between, when her
daughter growing too young and beautiful,
came vulnerable looking for love. She
spewed silk-swaddled crickets in her ears,
from her silky castle in the sky. Said she
wasn't fast or friendly enough
and they had to be best friends. Venom
splayed on child's back walking out.

She fell hard into the winter of old age,
her aloneness growing wild to the sky.
Her elder heart doing somersaults,
instead of peacefully settling into the flow
of a river's wisdom. Longing to go back
in time, she eyed her daughter trying to
reach across constellations of belief
past austere ancestors, wade wide waters
to muddy banks to see what the world
was made of, dance across dark fields
of moonlit blossoms of what may be
to see if she could outsmart her family
ghosts, while Mom told her how great
her sister was doing.

The Owl

An owl perched high in viridescent frills.
Seeing who walked into the world,
without them knowing it.

In a tree above, like a little God.

Good Hiding Spot

The child hid to be
herself for a while
without the world
telling her who she
was or shouldn't be.
She wandered wide and afar
across the world and time,
without an airplane or wings.
Down a moment of wisdom
who knew the old world back
when it was water on canvas,
before mountains began to rise.
An eminent crystal she
must half-cover because
a dragon could steal
the sun aglow and
miracles grew
like fire there.

The Crinkling Trees

Starved and naked,
trees dwell down in the dirt,
in the dark. They reach
for birds' eggs to eat at night,
drop dead sticks, drumming
to the crackling rhythms
of bones.

They stay up late and dance
under a whole moon until
dawn with owls and spiders.
Hide away opossums and bats
and other homely animals,
where light doesn't catch
and where gnarls and fangs
are too sharp to rest
in the soul of the eye.

For a great part of the year, trees
happily dance and smile a lot.
They love the light. Normally,
butterfly wings and netted stars
dress oaks' hundred-year-old skeletons
away from eyes. But an October tree
is indifferent to the sun
being gone.

Knotted branches tauntingly
crinkle the sky.

The Beautiful Wound

If I could only show you a photograph of her
from before she met my father.
Her dark brown hair long and thick
like a horse's mane, her eyes were wide
laughing at you and the earth.

I'd sit down with her to find surprise
in her eyes and enigmatic life she
couldn't share bursting inside. She
knew what I was going to say
already, what I felt before I did,
hiding deep in the long grasses,
amused to watch your lips speak
with courage.

She had a shovel with the right questions
to dig out the heart. I'd end up telling her
everything. Then she said nothing,
gave my personal prayers as gifts
to the birds.

I wonder, what do you know?
I bet you know power, but I mean
about pain, and empathy and joy,
and the deep roots of humanity in
earth and what layers of earth went first.
I wonder, do you know how to listen,
for something saturated in wisdom
and meaning—

listen, when this great earth and God
are trying to tell you something.

Scribbles of a Child

In the bathroom,
her legs dangling high
off the ground, off
a tree. Clipboard in lap,
pencil in hand.
She felt the moment,
round and sensuous, ready to
stretch into a mountain.
From the depths of her sea,
the tasty worth of the human soul
on her fingers and lips.
Lost in the hearts and minds
of others, she gathered herself in
with a fishing net, sailing
to the ends of the earth
not by boat but by
what is invisible and
free of form,
squeezing with the wind,
between the cracks, flying
with the freedom of birds.
Her scribbles pouring out,

meaning more than words.

I sometimes want to cry for a child
with a lost childhood.
Then try to find where all the lost childhoods go.
But they are probably hiding somewhere,

out playing hide-and-seek by now.

Forest Tents

Spidery home so tightly woven,
suffocates the branch and leaves
so they crawl to the ground and
beg God to begin again. Like the
home plopped down in the middle
of the enchanted forest we ran
through as kids, flattening the earth
like a pancake. The air, life, and
water unable to breathe beneath.
Forgotten was the soft silk thread
made of stars sewn into fingertips
meant to mend and the promise
to always make the world a better
place.

Looking Back in a Broken Mirror

Father drove in a rusty truck, with a
hole eaten out by a rat in the floor,
with gold coins heaping in the bed
his world didn't tender. He worked
all day until sunset, like a plow horse
with a saw and hammer to fix what
was broken in homes. The farmhouse
of his youth wasn't ever fixed, with
corn growing to treetops before it could
be shucked, booze running down his
father's throat like water, television
running as dream in the children's sleep.
Nor were the hearts of his four brothers
sleeping on a twisted mattress on the floor
he did not wish to wake going to the toilet,
under a roof of midnight stars. His
father nursed the bottle, wailing you ain't
no good for nothing at the child
in the mirror.

II.

Hard Wake

I lay on a bed of plywood,
my heart running sprints in sleep.

I crawl out on my elbows and knees.
The sun above, my eyes on the dirt.

I am a lunar moth
with a tear in my glassy wing,
hanging onto life with one eye.

Pond of Leaves

The sheen of the hollow sun reflects on
the pond of leaves. Foliage and grass hibernate
with the bears and crawl to silence.
A mushroom burgeoned into a balloon sleeps
with the fish in the winter who crawl with fins
into stillness.

The breeze looks winter in the eye and laughs.
The glassy mirror ruffles in the breeze.
The wind pays no attention to winter.
Its life is passage, wafting the lives it ruffles
and lithely touches. It plucks what's ripe
before it leaves.

Patches of fertile trails scamper into statues
of forest. They quicken to the speed of light
in a curse, marks what used to be with red ink.

In Illness

There's a time to be restful, drop all your
matters, look at the world in repose
sigh. At this time, the only motion should
be ceasing, falling in the depths of the
meandering hour of a long, past century,
like bears who rest their grand weight,
dormant all winter.

There's a pain that manifests in a feral body,
swollen in the interwoven waters of earth.
A body of self who won't make music,
whose feet won't dance, arms won't lift,
legs won't carry, whose mind won't think
and heart won't love—a body that knows
no other clarity than its pain. From then on,
a ghost of the body walks with you,
who carries the sensitivity of life and the world,
who will never not know what bodies do
to be a body.

In these times, would you remember to
take your body, hold it in your arms,
sing to it ballads and verses, carry it
by the good times of corporal memory,
as far and as long as you can go.

Cold Spell

The cold nipped fingertips raw.
It stole the feeling from toes
and turned lips gangrene purple.
Froze the fiery ball to look
more like the moon,
and swept small bits of life
into a cavernous wind tunnel,
without a chance to say a wish.
The cold snapped ice crystals
from thin air, chasing us into our
warm, cozy houses.
The spell embalmed trees forever
like pharaohs, froze animals
in animation, waking great sleeping
bear with its arctic whisper,
and sweeping its silky breath
across barren blankets. It froze
the ground solid through
and through, oceans into opaque
glass, snatched the song from
the bluebirds and chickadees with
high hopes the butterflies and geese
made it to the sun's front yard.

In the Dark

Each day I awoke
with a different throat,
my throat clutching a cleaver's knife,
my neck mortared with bricks,
my hands and legs curled up
in a wound. I couldn't see past

eyes of morning fog. Even so,
I arose shuffling my soles
over simmering coals, my calves
bearing the weight of the world,
my stomach kicked in with horse hooves
though I never walk behind horses.
Hunched over, my eyes peeled on the dirt,

looking at how life changes into rich soil,
I went down the stairs to search for the harp
to play my body's music, hips popping balloons,
knees knocking loose change, turning around
forgetting where I was going,
barbs burrowed my bones with quills.

I wondered if I could be imagining this,
then every patch of pain pink,
as if God were saying, no!

I tried everything, holding onto each hope
in my hand in the beginning,
my hand empty in the end. I followed
everyone who said I know the way,
everyone I followed did not.

Years did not loosen its noose,
my body fought my body in another
battle, as always in war
both sides lost.

There was nothing left to try,
I arranged my pile of knotty sticks,
useless to me now, built a fort
out of them. Nothing left to do,
I watched life through slowly
closing grieving fingers
as butterflies flew off to life
without me. My symbiotic harp
lost in the field of human frailty
underneath a rose garden
of taut flesh.

She saw the ends of sweet roots
with the earth's riches
of gold secrets and dark stars.

An image of herself would have
walked by.

Night Sleeps

In a shadow of the soul,
it's too dangerous to
live meaningfully.
The night takes the lives it wants,
who will not go to the next day.

I hear the quiet of dark against a sunny promise.
The day lives one way.
The night stays up one way.
The moon, sun, and earth align,
pulls upon you. Hearts slow
in dreams we may not forget,
dancing in beds at night,
with eyes closed blind,
head held toward the deep ground,
in reverence to everything I do not know.

Still alive, when you thought you may
never see your old friend
beautiful soul again.

Ears to the Sky

I have seen a rabbit freeze for a
bull snake. Fear can take over life
like rabbits' long ears to the sky,
heart rapid, too afraid to breathe,
not afraid of death, but of something
more scary, life without living.
When I wished my body would brim
with bravery, my body did the
opposite, let worry shrivel and dry up
the prayer of robust life in the throat,
like a prune, collapsed inward,
dehydrated, wondering how to be,
unlike the sun or rock or tree, who
breathes to the eternal beat; not with
robust hues and vigor but fear.
I remember being in front of the cold
gray stares of speech class, face a
tomato, the pools under arms, voice
gone too far back in the throat,
a wish to go down a rabbit hole
and live between safe, loving walls
of a womb. I am afraid and I am brave,
I tell myself, to give my suffering
back in another form.

My Body Lay

My body lay in a puddle of pain,
unable to play the body's music,
my song somewhere lost
within my plumy throat and
dancing legs and arms reaching
hands holding life by the wheel,
and mouth pulling from a
deep, enchanting ribbon,
with my mind's missing keys,
and heart attuned. So I
relearned, note-by-note,
how to be a body,
my sore throat to swallow,
my legs to travel, my arms reaching
hands holding life like a precious
rock found on the ground as a child.
My mouth to sing myself to sleep,
a lullaby afloat among the hills
in ribbons of sun, my eyes to hold
the memory of a working body,
forgotten in a field where
angels and children play.

Dream

She sat up her body from bed.
Rinsed her organs out with a hose.
Hung her muscles out to dry,
with the rays and wind airing them out.
Combed the disease from her tissue.
Tweezed out any last remnants
from her brain.

Then she wiped away her lost time
and memory of the world
ready to discard her in a swipe of
a bug. Nabbed bits of bravery
from the deer living at home with wolves.
Fight from storm's winds reaching
its fist around trees. Buzz from
crickets on marshes edge,
announcing summer is here.

Took the stairs two-by-two to days
that were excited to be alive.
Cycled across the country
when the bed tried to catch her.
Took a bite of the sun.

That woke her up.

Reason for Suffering

I told my body I'd be happy anyways—
engaged every sinew
to make my eyes as bright as eyes,
my voice as present as the sun,
the shards of spine to stand up straight.

I was still waiting for the answer to
what is the reason for suffering,
for the moon to unfold its silk petals into why,
when I fell asleep standing up
before the stars had time to sing a lullaby.

These little words were already written.
I can't change them even if I tried.
The moon would know.
The sun would put out a strong arm and say stop.
The sea's waves would rise and override them,
surely rise and overthrow them
to intimidate me to be a scribe
for what the atmosphere wants to say, what is in the air,
what is silence but has never been given life
what has never been given sound in words or
in music, the most beautiful order of sound.
Only if we listen with our eyes and ears and nostrils,
those words are thrown upon us.

III.

Life Waiting on a Park Bench

In life, it is clear some things were meant
to be. In the dark you must feel them
with the lights off by your gut. In dim
light, I'm lost with an upside-down
map going where I don't know. I reclaim
a little, when I stop and look at the flowers
within the flower I never saw before.
I wonder what's been here all along
like love everywhere, and what world
exists and what this world can be,
questions of the thinking heart
whose answers are found in old books.

The things that are right are old from
childhood. They come to you like a lion.
If someone asks if they should do
something, they probably shouldn't.
They must restore the gut to see bears
and bunnies and know what to do.
It's the gut that walks you to your life
waiting on a park bench, rising so tall
and large. The new things look small
and diminished, flat without the life
inside. I fall out of life into a wetland
of puddles. Walk up the stairs, trying to
find the door where I left off. I trip over
rocks and want to talk without saying
a thing.

Lost

Without a brain she walked
down the street, looking for her
mind in a mouth or behind a trash-
can. She remembered in gray fog
when they came the morning before
and snatched it in a dream.

She tried her hardest to think it back,
to harness her life in its grainy form.
The wonderful memories of mediocre
times, bland memories of unbelievable
turns. The people who loved her
she didn't know did, the people she loved
ever so whom didn't know her. The thought
skeletons that frame life, for emotion to fill
home with light.

Tried her darndest to scrape it out
from underneath the horse's hoof.
Pull it down with some twine from
flying in a cloud. Shake it off after
sitting saturated in a puddle of mud.
It eager to fly to another,
as a butterfly of wisdom, intuition
or a funny thought seed
to blossom into a tree.

A Bug

She felt inanimate
like an empty teacup.
Longing to live in
humbleness and beauty.
But existing as a shriveled bug,
too ugly and stupid
to show one eye.

Foreign Accent

The girl too weary of life sounded foreign
to people. Whatever it was,
her low coarse voice, like barley,
barren with wind, without song
and summer. Her gestures, her mannerisms
between the throes of joy and tragedy.
The strange thoughtful things she said
in an artful flow of river,
after a long pause of honesty.
On a wave between the mind and heart,
stretched to another moon.

Stories

Stories may hold life by the teeth, you know,
tucked away like stolen pieces of truth,
delivered from a mouth or movement,
or lack of song or movement,
or shadow from long ago.

Stories packed away in the bodies cavities.
The closets, crannies, wherever
room may be. Beneath the right
shoulder or in the heart,
when like a hollow tree
or without blossom
to attract the bees.

We often must break to heal,
stories opening down rivers,
pooling into red seas in knees
or in the soles of bottoms
of feet like little fish. Stories
abridged into little moments,
separating from the origin,
pouring out into the sky,
absorbed by love and light,
tucked in small pockets of wind
that can soothe and mend into
a silky strand of an earful of hope.

Mistaken Sisters of the Queen

The women stayed in a constellation
with the worth of every silver star.
Eyeing the soaking girl in the river
without extending a daisy
from their field. The baby toe
of their heart too occupied
to dip in the sea of humanity.
They wore neat new outfits of
perfection that didn't match
humanness made of earth and sea.
When the dirt ground wouldn't,

their image carrying their soul,
sparkling on a road of eyes.

What if perfection, with its straight skinny line
and cold stern face, was wrong all along?

What if it only tricks lives in its direction
and begs people to come and stay
because it's cold and lonely
and needs more life to buy it time,
but it spends its capital too quickly,
because the joy and love hang out of
perfection, because they lived
and got their hands dirty?

High Horse

The woman's eye winked as their shirts' sweat
clung. Her nose high on a horse, she didn't
mind seeing hearts choke. Her eyes beat on
the private space of a person before she put
it on a list for later. Between us and them,
she kept them guessing who was us flat on
a line. Folded her deficiencies and
vulnerabilities into others' misfortunes and
misgivings. Everything else she didn't understand she drank before going to bed at night. A
smile in the eyes and face as they glimpsed to
see if a human was human.

Outside Walls

The ways of the ruthless world, surely, won't
change. Our bodies will follow what looks like
love to almost anything. We have always trudged
through the mud, rain, and snow to survive.
We reside in a storm of turmoil and bliss,
between bookends. The rest of life is a matter
of arranging and rearranging things in pecking
order because the open landscape is intimidating.
An infinity of doors open to the same place and
go anywhere. It's based on a strong man, a loud
voice, and red sweaters and shoes. Of course, there
is no order. We each are different and stand out.
Our spirit is a catching mitt for essences of
stories. We each are the same earth, water,
fire, and air.

Inside walls, you learn to see the system.
Outside, you learn to become unafraid of
how much you know.

The Empty Woman People Loved

She pasted a clown smile on her face
in the frames of doors
and coughed lovely words
in a sing-song voice
that sounded good
in the echoes of her voice to
ingratiate ears.

It worked, deep in her heart
was a lion who ordered
the jungle by color
and hunted birds for fun
to fill the shadow of
her soul. At home
a moment alone, empty,

she left, for affirmation
of who she was.

Cough, Stand

The earth actually wants you to cough,
stand up, walk out, say,
I'm not comfortable with this,
giving no reason why.

The earth roots for wise and loving courage,
emanating in echoes across land masses,
reverberating in ripples across expanse,
over peaks and valleys, sweeping in the wind
across breathfuls of blue.
To lost, faraway ears,
or a heart, homeless,
somewhere lost,
flying in a cloud.

Soulful Bearings

The soft animal must fight to survive in this world.
It's buried under the muddle, rubbish, and gadgets
in disbelief it exists.
The gut keeps singing about the windy reservoir
that knows what you know before you know.
Your mind catches up to admit it was there
and reason profundity.

Under fluorescent smiles,
the soul is a wilting dandelion.
It is a bunny that stays still under the nose
of a high horse.
Its fondest wish is to sit in a chair,
without being poked or chided,
and rise when it wants to rise
and fall when it's time
and not listen to drama humanity
holds onto.

Sometimes it retreats in a turtle shell,
but I say get out there, and breathe
the fresh air.
Who else is it for?

A Thousand Setting Suns

In youth, I was fond of the feral beauty of the wolf,
until I saw the deer carcasses scattered like shells
in the sand. They always got the peaceful deer
in the ecstatic party of the moonlight. I liked
the boundless sea, which always triumphed
human activity in immediate greatness, but not
its tumultuous waters that engulfs ships and
vessels and swallows things whole.

This is the human condition, I once thought,
to love and hate the same world all at once,
the same moment, place, time, and self,
to resist partition and forge all sides
together from an ancient act of bravery.
That mysterious place in the human spirit
where exists the root of all things,
like tenacity, gentleness of heart
and a thousand setting suns.

This Day

Even when a shadow of distress
tries to dry my resilience
and steal my wellspring,
the wind's cool soul fills this old house.
I hear the children's sweet voices,
each as a different wildflower.
Surely, when I leave this earth,

I will begin to understand something.

IV.

Wait for White

For many months sometimes I wait,
I wait for something to happen,
for the white doves to swoon in.
But the day is still, the sun is still,
it is cold and browned.
Leaves of last summer lie as a
blanket on the forest floor.
I don't mind the decay,
but I do wonder where spirits go,
if they get lost or find the
heavenly place or did they find
a burrow or a hole in a tree
once inhabited by a pileated
woodpecker, that dragon bird
like the giant swallowtail fluttering
out of the pages of a fairytale,
or do they go to sleep or follow on
the heels of loved ones, trying to
whisper one last thing, surrounding
them by love.

The Gray Day

A day the sun shines gray and salt-flavored wind
all the way from the sea fills my eyes with tears,
when I was looking to see the sun.
The green grass will come out in a dream,
when the chill of winter extinguishes like fire,
in a world that is far, that I cannot see now.
The landscape doesn't hold the comfort for beauty.

Oh, where is the prayer, the confidence
of yesterday?

Belief

I went sifting through the world for the answer,
sawing down trees and picking wildflowers
to look at their roots. Others didn't need to know.
They were buoyed up by faith by a foot,
wrapped in bows of bliss, praising God for
their gifts. God had a path for their life,
others with belief also. They healed themselves
and each other by listening with belief like a
fixed star, had a future flight to leave this
world on wings of faith, for one
draped in white with only good horses
and perfect love and loved stars too early lost.
Hands stretched straight to God.
Eyes attracted to them like magnetic poles,
trying to see the God they knew, belief
held with the familiarity of a best friend.

The Top

We walked to the top of the wild
with freedom pressing our faces,
and glee off birds' wings
fallen into our mouths. I wonder
from where inspiration comes,
loosely afloat in the raw air,
ready to kiss wide open ears,
painting children with brushes
the colors of a promise,
surely it dives and dips freely
as a bird and cares greatly.

I saw God
who sat in an idyllic sky,
in the crystal clarity
of my child's eye.
There a threshold of celestial light,
an angelic cloud, wistful white across
perfect azure, mighty walls around
His heavenly garden,
angels standing guard.

Hug the Tree

She knelt in a bed of snow,
before a tree, wishing
it were God that she could
meet in this life and be
reassured of good.
Only to cry for the rest
of her life from both joy
and relief, that our world
is as beautiful as we
imagine.

Then a voice inside says,
open your eyes, you are
constantly reassured of
good and beauty.

I'd be so beside myself,
I would forget to eat,
starving, to hug a tree.

Gray Wolves

The gray wolf may still rule the night.
They show teeth and bark so everyone
parts the sea when they pass. But
under luminous sunrays and during
happy celebration, they scrunch in a
stump, disappear under the dirt,
or fly in the sky behind a cloud.
The genuine smiles are too loud
and bright for the dark shadow in
their eye.

For a while, we don't have to see
or think of them, we carry on
happily with our lives. For all we know
they may have boarded a flight for
another world. But when we do see
them, our fence full of flowers grows
higher and stands taller. We hear
echoes of their tribal yodels in the
clearing around cries of poor
surrounded prey, and bear our teeth
large.

The gray wolf is gone those times.

The Night Shivers

Much like the frozen lake.
The avid crystals light
my face fresh. Frigid
silhouettes bend across
the wintry road.
I wonder
how far

the black night
goes back, if a light
so bright is behind
to make the black so black.
Each life is
an enigmatic gift

wrestling the translucent wind,
scooping up efflorescence
from frosty furled leaves,
rendering the silk filament
between night
and day.

The Question You Have

Some people have more than their share
of suffering, and like the world, it's kind of

a saga—solemn and deep like a shipwreck.
Steadying readying to rise to kissed waters

with a fortified bow and stern, next time
to sail upon deep breath, shrug, because

she wasn't there yet. The world wasn't willing
to face the vulnerable human heart yet.

It's always swallowed itself, with a whale gulp,
a forceful lunge, a malign rock inside readying

to send out soldiers to defeat itself, steadying
readying to rise with a fortified bow and stern,

this time to sail upon deep breath, this time
with a sparkling laugh, a melodious song,

an artful prayer, to sail upon God's deep breath.

Brush Wolf's Resolve

The brush wolf's spirit inhabited
her body when she chose
the path few walked upon.

The opossums, going back and forth,
on whether it's fair to get a chicken,
stopped. The worms writhing
inside finally stilled.
Instead of the world
moving a breeze,
her boulder limbs,

moved life around,
like there was no other way to go,
than the way she was going.

Wringing a Rag

Wringing her hands dry
in the sink. Through
a cleft of trees,
the twinkling starface
of God.

She pours hibiscus tea
in morning prayer
for her life.

Furtive and meaningful,
always about to blossom, waiting
waiting until she
becomes honest.

The Great Spring Thaw

The slope with twig and leaf impressions
in sodden clay, rain remnants in the air,
moss cuddling up around oak feet, velvet
green carpets trees walk upon.

A last spartan patch of winter left, the little
snow clings to earth upon its return, like a
lone cottony sheep longing for its flock
on rainy blue fields.

A melting pond kisses the shore, bullying the
land back just a nudge. Before the land knows it,
more waters rising, anxious to come in
to stretch out for more room. The great land
pushes back to hold onto itself in certainty,
knowing all you can do is have in your heart
your rapturous joy and inspiring views,
your reasons to push back your hardest
for the time being and to hold on and push
more when the next storm comes.

After her life washed away in a rainfall.
She wondered why she had been so scared.
When all she could see were flowers growing
in a sea of fire.

The Small Bunny of the Wood

They don't choose a gilded cage.
The small bunny of the wood chooses
the wild. The world where beavers
by their own volition in earnest play
to build up brokenness. The wood
where wolves mercilessly hold throats
between ivory fangs, and pleasurefully
taste berries' sweet juices. Where
flowers and leaves of goldenrod
and plantain grow, with the capacity to
heal humanity. Where we tread on
moss carpets with sharp silver slivers,
under hawks' claws uncoiling from the sun.
Where the sun shines on all things,
no matter how deserving.

The earth with wind that swirls
cloud, twig, and bird
into a glorious sky's open mouth.

Fence of Foliage

I used to live in a world where everyone was good and smart.
Darkness on earth didn't exist, and if I looked upon it,
it was my fault.
The world brandished its fists, banged my head into a brick wall,
stealing my words, artifacts, and some life, saying,
define what you mean by good.

I crawled into a safe shell to protect the soft material of the heart,
asking a wise elder to sit with me
to consider wounds.
I had thought, didn't humanity have enough in common?
I brought in voices of good people all from different lives
who knew smartness, and I saw
their strong nets made of love, to catch
them as they fall.

The thick walls obscured the wingspans of great birds
soaring over the treetops on a sky growing gold.
I shed the thick shell and grew a living fence of foliage,
woven comfortably and strongly on a landscape
with room for rain and sun.
I could listen very closely for music or an ear for walking away,
handout the shapes of foliage in words,
to ask them to stay or go, move or dance.
I would add taller trees and bushes with thorns for wolves
and strangers. I neatly tended this garden
that sounded like a silent river
and looked like gentle wind.

Walking into Their World

I walk in, to formally dine in their world.
It tips and turns. I relax,
then a gun is pointed at my head.
That's life, I say,
and I keep walking. But I still wonder
what is the world?

I'd like to sculpt it into pure goodness and love.
It appears not easily malleable.
The sea rolls, easily and calmly
and tumbles violently. I look to it.
Going back, there is the circus.
It's tempting to be pulled in, to begin dancing.
The cool air flows wine and rapturous ideas.
Backwards, I trip back to the puddles of the moon.

V.

The Precious Table

A lifetime after, across the seas and time,
she chopped my precious table's legs off,
without asking, she knew what the answer
would be, put it in her living room, as a
centerpiece, a sacrifice to her God.

The remnants of the table, what soul
is left, I have it back now, gathered in
my womb, as a promise to love and
nurture the children always.
The table is torn and tattered, but loved.
It is broken like a colt by humanity who
desperately longs to reign itself back in,
but not enough to meet its true self.

Looking, I see its original beautiful self
in a vision, the old soulful way truth
emerges in breathfuls from wild freedom,
for hearts to fly.

Dead Life

Trees tall statues.
Cattails bowing slightly forward.

The sky was a frozen azure lake
and dead silent.

But there was more there
than what she felt, dead.

Then, a little life of the sky on
her breath. A bit of life of the trees
in her ear and mouth, then eye,
awash over her skin.

The life off the land on her fingers
and in her hands once again.

The Slow Song

The day I awoke,
there was no pain in the world.
The thread had been between
my fingers all along. It was a day
angels did the chores and made
the bed. My mother used to say,
tomorrow is a new day! as if
each new day was a new life.

No worms manifested, writhing
in guts, no wolf jaws ripping up
throats like leaves.
No devil horns peaking around
the corner ready to take children
heart and soul away from parents
unless they hid under the bed
Godspeed. No brooding music
up at midnight to play once more,
to frighten away happiness, but
the spirit of joy waiting in casual
clothes for the heart to accept,
to spoon it softly out like pudding
and pluck at time's strings to
make little miracles.

That day I looked away
at the happy little brook,
taking its time.
To laugh and have fun
and fully bask
in a stream of light.
There was no pain,
no death in the world too.

Sinking House

She pulled herself out with twiggy arms
and wings from a house sinking in a swamp
of feces overflowing from life full of down-
pour. Prayed for the world to lend her peace,
when its sneeze shattered her like fine china.

Calm just for a moment, between azure sky
and twinkling sea, family shadows stayed
stubbornly on her like warts, when about
to release as a majestic butterfly to flutter
in the wild to eternal happiness.
With brains alit like a firefly on her back
and life she half-made up.

Become the Person You Were

Become the person you were that day.
That day when you were seven.
When your body decided to walk away from the world
like a shadow does at sunset.
When you picked your life course, on a frivolous breeze,
like picking out a hair style, you got used to
and forgot you could change,
until you sat and looked at your familiarity,
and didn't recognize it at all.
Much meaning is done in silent work like this
from the soul end.

You took a different way than you were going,
and left your self behind. Waiting many years,
like the strong one waiting in love,
going on with your life
but in a beautiful silent way not needing hope,
but never fully giving up hope,
as you started a new life as someone else,
and left the right one behind.

Courage

From the thorns in his family's field
he walked with his values and ideals,
across a jungle war.
Romance draining
in rivers of blood
into the next life,
walking deaf into
a cloud of love.
He pounded
dead trees for supper,
working labor into peace,
the world growing deliciously
in strangeness.

Light in his azure
eyes still sparkling seas.

Early Morning

Silver sheathes of grass,
bowed to God in flocks.

Clover flowers, often houses
of harbinger lights, listing
on open water. Leaves,
still stumbling drunk
from beads of rain.

Whispers from Meaningful World

It was whispering too loud,
trying to get my attention,
interrupting a world
that insisted it was real,
even controlled the silence
in pauses.
I noticed too late
that I shrugged that other world off,
the meaningful one that dances
to the rhythm of magic and the moon.

The Brush Wolf

His eyes stolen by wild.
I saw his presence before his coat
of gray bark.
He was an omen and a blessing.

I stepped toward him, wondering who he was.
He rose gracefully, holding the sacred ground
with the strength and dignity of a good leader,
staying in place
knowing who loves the earth more.

His eyes feasted on what he could of a foreign species,
and without another thought to humanity
disappeared into the white garden of heavenly trees,
to follow the wild beauty home.
Neither submitting nor yielding upon great impasse,
his superiority and strength held humbly in his belly,
his movements neither more hurried
nor more languid
than a creature attuned to the moon.

From Treetops

Bluebirds and warblers sing,
vultures squawk and exclaim,
fly off as they wish.

Where do they fly?
They fly to exotic places
with warm sun, wondrous views,
other skies and worlds.

Then, what do they do?
They go home.

Inner Land

When she couldn't find her innermost land.
She had nothing. She didn't know what
the trees were doing in the wind.

She didn't know who the sun was.
All the beaver did was work.
The bees bumbling along stalks
of grass looked lost.

She looked up in the sky and saw
nothing. She wondered,
what was the purpose?

When she looked from the light
of her moon, the trees were dancing.
She saw the sun shined on her
and everything on earth.

The beaver was playing with sticks
in the water. Blossoms whom the
bees visited were good friends.
The sky was more vibrant
than anything.

The world was too inspired
for a reason.

Seals off the Coastline

The barks of seals.
Numerous as deer
on a polished boulder.
A short haven away from
razor-sharp entrapment.

From tiny jagged cliffs,
crowns wading in wet glass
look up. The unblinking
soulful eyes that walk
back time.

I see you, they say.

We see humanity
and the complexity of living
a domesticated wild heart.

His Favorite Armchair

A good day's work done. All work still
heaped, piling high to the sky
each evening, relaxing playing chess
watching an old show,
in front of the wood burning stove.
Between duty is beauty and agony.

The agony comes from knowing the soul.
Its long reach for eternity and love. It lives as a
stranger in the human world, where the body meets
the idea of pain in reconciliation forever.
The beauty, it's mostly in moments of sensitive
human hearts, when there is everything to lose
and nothing to gain. It's in the robust design
of the earth and everything it blossoms.
The music of the land, wind, sun, air,
and rain. The imagination in the sinuous trees,
greenish grasses, rising mountains, and rolling seas.

While relaxing it all disappears,
sitting in his favorite armchair.

The Day

The doctor said the
infection had spread like
minnows in red rivers.
Dad worked and played
in peaceful meadows, under
lambent rays, all the same.

He didn't clamber for a breath,
like the midge's fight for dryland
on water's edge. The vine's sprint
to the treetops for a crumble of
sun. The rabbit's rocket from jaws
and teeth.

He thought of life and the world
in the same quality. Remembered
to take another breath, long and
deep between the sun and sea.
With the heart, not the mouth,
drawing from the earth's midst.

Wouldn't quit playing unless
the bed ate him.

The Ghost Herds

I dream fondly of what the prairie grass-
lands looked like so long ago.
Only slivers of grass seas left,
where ghost herds of bison rumble the
blond dewy mist. Hunchback beasts bow
and toss the sky closer to the sun.
They matte winter earth dusted with
dandruff, stampede clumps of spiked hair
into skullcap, cold cigar puffs
from nostril caverns.

They roam summer's fairy-sized land
with salamander spirits bolting like slithery deer
and freezing like still gray rock. Myriad grass-
hopper ghosts boomerang off grass blades
over the moon. Bull snake memories bask
in echoes of sun, churning on the thirsty earth
a sign of infinity, among prairie leaned by wind.

Never settling until the land runs golden
and the bison dancing on wild blue horizon,
mold into their animated architecture,
from clay again.

Fields of Quiet

When I didn't need
music to fill vast deserts of emptiness.
Silence cooed, like a meandering river,
full of dense miracles and stars.
If I listened patiently enough
I would hear flowers sing,
as they danced in the breeze
and maybe if I'm lucky,
God's voice whispering

everything will be all right.

Hopefully these short words of spoken music
just don't get lost.
They rise up, past the clouds,
as seeds planted in fields of sky,
blossoming to augment the peace
of the moon.

If She Doesn't Write

If she doesn't write and empty her brain
of the world, like a teapot. Life is a dragon,
she runs from. One bouncy step ahead of
a sad sea, angry fire, or loving sun
in a shadow. Clinging to a moment
she knew like an old friend, a possibility
of what may be true.

Heart to Hand

I translate my heart with my hand,
in words made of silent notes and
laughter spilling out windows
and soft tears purring in the shadows.
It's like tuning into an old song
painting words on an open canvas
before you, across the sun and night,
the hilltop and ravine. Life that is easily
missed between windy prayers
and cries for more. I try to carefully
understand what the old moon says
to the rhythmic rocking of the sea,
what shaped the drifting continents
before you or I were born.
I write to life, begging it to stop
playing hide-and-go-seek,
to land its meaning in the middle,
stop just for a moment,
so I can find the words.

VI.

The Empty Fence

The barbed-wire fence originally
kept the cows in, before
the people with their heritage
and machetes came.

We were told that morning
before breakfast. That afternoon
we watched out the window
but didn't.
We talked in our usual voices
but it was quiet.
We eventually went over
to the burial pits.
All the land and animals
were silent.
The tree branches
did not move.
No birds were in the sky.
It was light out but with
no shine.

I remember wondering if
for every death
the earth did this.

Feral Screech of Guinea Fowl

For a whole moon,
the brush wolf and fox paced.
On the outside
of an invisible pocket full of air,
in the peace and quiet.

Staving off death
another moment.
The wild polka-dotted screech foreign
to them, from the yawning jaws
of a lion.

Blossoms by the Bed

Every day she pulled petals from
sunsets and picked up off the
ground what had fallen off
angels' wings.
Every day she gave him every-
thing in her basket.
Every day they placed the blossoms
beneath the bed because they knew
blossoms never opened
under the moon.

If it's not arranged in a journal,
does it exist?
She caught his last breath in her fist.
Before he slipped out of his eyes
into a field where the soul finds wings,
and blossoms open
like love emitting from eyes
a blind man can see,
wild truth blowing
children's hair in the wind,
never letting up.

Shells on Rotted Log

Seashell families forced to leave
their home of blue,
settled on the next
best thing.

On rotten fallen
trees growing
miraculously into thriving
clans as numerous
as stars, changing
a little to live.

Every Child Has an Icon

I watched my father closely that perfect day,
with a few simple words,
he put together a world,
who saved me
from the insanity
that reaches with its claws
every moody hour, every child has an icon.
In my memory,
he always had a handsome chiseled face,
like a rock,
was tall and tan,
and exuded the strength and peace
an angel had given him,
because the world would not.
He built a new world from a penny,
most of his life he was drowning,
never learned how to swim,
for him to always walk up onto the shore,
and say this is what I've always wanted.
I stood next to him that summer day,
almost the last one
when it's clinging to time before change,
he was leaning casually on the car,
fading back into the earth,
chatting as though we had every day left
in the world to live
every day for me to tell him
he was my icon.

Here I am, talking to God,
trying to say something beautiful,
and explain in words

that this is the perfect summer day,
the sun was happy,
but not hot,
the wind's breath was present,
but not cool.
He is still here,
as real as I imagine him.

Antique Cedar Table

I dragged the table, I stained and cooed
and lauded over, and praised
and worshipped, down the uneven lip of the garage.
The snaking wooden legs must have squeezed it
to death. I saw the work of a lifetime go
unrecognized, a fusty cloud of old poison
settling in the cracks and crevices.

A table is a meeting place,
where our souls pour out our secrets,
loneliness and compulsions
in burps and chokes in between words.
We must sit, tied to the chair of our commitment
until we say goodbye for the rest of our lives
and nobody loves that.
We say goodbye all the time forever,
and deeply know it.

I don't trick myself into thinking
I won't see him again soon. Scale over a mountain
flank, pass through the open field over the
white farm fence,
in timing of his coming,
in the foliage and trees thick of forest,
trip on a tree branch,
I will fall and there he will be.

A deaf world looks away from death.
It doesn't care to drink from healing waters of wells
or place foliage to draw out the wound.

It keeps on. Lifts the sun high with strong arms.
Blows a round silver moon far away with every breath
it takes.

Bugs the Giant Steps On

I used to cry at night for the baby bunny
left ravaged by the housecat
along the dirt path
beaten by my brother's running bare feet.
When I almost stepped on it,
to hurt it more. Do you remember
what it was like to be a child,
to think about all the bugs
you, the giant, must step on to get from
one place to the next?
All those soft, dewy thoughts,
ready for adventure?
A few hours going on
to last a lifetime?

My father spoke economically,
as if you lose words each time you speak.
He said, it's a part of life.

Rain

I don't love storms, the rumbling thunder
coming closer close, louder loud.
The outpouring of relief, the letting, when
the earth expels anger or grief or joy.
The pouring of the rain clouds onto the crops,
to the lake basins, the sweeping hills, the low
valleys, the old mountains settling into themselves.

Before a storm, I crank the old oak window,
smell the air's energy, quickening
like sweet violet. Over the house,
a dark cloud cast, fingers unfolding,
reaching for eternity, and there were
no suns. A world without sun,
could you imagine?

The storm comes in through the open
window in a redirection of energy,
the world comes in.
Rain, a prayer for the animals,
and land, and people,
for the healing and regrowth of the world,
for the healing regrowth of humanity,
the levity and upswell of breadth,
the land so impressible
and soft like lambs wool.

The Bloody Feather

That bloody feather is a wound
mixed with wind. Churning
on dampened grass, with
straw, twig, and moss.
Touched down to settle,
uptaken, renewed in spirit.
The favorite they always
knew. Too alive abundant
in joy, deserving more
time on earth, loved life
just as any. Went to see the
caretaker to visit the house.
His scrappy presence and
joy, a sapling nursed
back to health, mangled
only further by world.
Fell to the precipitous
wild, but lives within.

Fallen Trees

All these dear fallen trees
lost on earth, found in spirit.

The Last Days of Summer

Amble slowly.
Trees doze off watching the world

on television in their favorite armchair.
Winds sweep the sun away with a witch's broom.

Meadows lay down for the sky
to hurl out white angels.

Leaves and petals flutter
past butterfly friends

hitching a ride on the wind
to the sun.

A restless little breeze,
not wanting to stay,

not wanting to go.

Fleeting Summer

Thud dropping from the sky.
The solidity of silence ringing ears.
Ended in a period.

After all, summer too must go.

Breath of Winter Forest

She breathes more clearly
in the woods, between
tapered sticks and vines
bending in rainbows of
thresholds to other worlds,
among felted clouds and
felled trees and trees
smooching the sky to be
robust and sparkling like
diamonds. Between trees
hugging and holding the
sun in close embrace like
a pirate's grip on a chest
full of gold.

The Crisp Fall Morning

This crisp fall morning
I wake up to the branches
splitting the sunrays.
I'm still grasping
what it is about this world
that is so vexingly beautiful.
The sun illuminates slight branches
as silver threads.
The heterogeneity of just the
leaf blanket on the forest floor,
say, we are all alike,
we are all unalike,
we are all beautiful.

It is the nature, the imagination,
the challenge,
the rest.

Show Yourself

There was a time in her life,
God asked, "Who are you?"

She stood up on her chair
and showed herself.

Squared up with the world.
Her failings let go, rain from the sky.
The petals she made held
out in a bouquet.

Nothing anyone said or did,
who didn't care, mattered.
But her gifts mattered,
her life growing blossoms in the sun,
which always found
the fields of creation most free.
Shedding the things that weren't her,
gains everything.

Morning Glass

Loons' wails of agony and joy.
Bounce across
still stubborn beauty.

The wind echoes the water.
Stretches its face
into a yawn of morning.

Textures of Beauty

We all must leave one sort of beauty for another.
The one we first knew to live in the real
kingdom that echoes in the flora of our gut
to the constant rhythm of the moon.
In the wood, the trees silently talk to each other,
not loud human voices that were never loud.
The rays of light wash over us through
the forest canopy.

Little virescent butterflies glued on branches
flutter in God's large fan in the sky.
The bush cascades down the clay banks of
the river.

Off the azure roof the children's voices echo sweet
happiness like the juice of black raspberries
that align the path, spreading into the thicket
for the birds and deer far beyond little fingers' reach.

The children gleam a few berries from the peripheral,
with absolute pleasure—
who better to notice, who better to experience
the goodness and beauty?

Who could think up all the delicate textures of beauty?

In Winter

Morning stars don't fall.
They linger in mid-air,
stop time,
and land in feathery echoes.

Windy country roads meander
shores of boulders spilled
by white-tipped ocean.

Dusted leaves scurry like mice,
across diamond-turned pond;
beneath, a woodpecker
hugs a tree,
jackhammers rot.

Faded rays faintly whisper
across snow-swept field.
Winters open blossom
in the air.

The Snow World

The snow with faces of fish scales
and dimples and acne
and clear baby skin.
White angelic butterfly wings
folding the continent.
Glimpse of heaven with animal stories,
transiently told,
in pellucid prints of life.

Hello, Stranger

The earth is longing to reach humanity,
always coming to greet us,
stepping forward with a cloud, as if to say,
hello, stranger,
let's get to know each other again.

VII.

Stories of Wind

Sea from a thousand miles
away fills the wind like the shell
held to a child's ear brimming
with story.

Stretching like a yawn into
sky, its coarse salt licks faces in
earth's wild, loving way.

Lying low a little,
resting among low open prairie.

Warm Secrets

Green life patient in prayer
through the long earth slumber.

Strand of wind twirls
dancing in silk whispers warm
secrets of summer.

A baby seed white rays sing to
shoots roots and stems to dark
and light. From an unfurling
bud a stem growing up to catch
fluttering blossoms.

The Clearing

The morning forest alive in the clearing.
Growling at young rabbits, give all.

Sacrifice
the silent moon of the heart.

World Child Created

A sweet blossom
growing up from sea to the blue.
Plays for hours in fields of eternity,
making the world what it ought
to be.

Already a loving mother to her
seven dolls, little voices playing
the piano, in a land full of fun
under peaceful stars. Tucking
them into bed with affirmation
and kisses of goodnight.

On the first day of school,
asks in wide-eyed surprise,
what is this world now?

The Black Boulder

Before nightfall the good mothers
brush their children's foreheads,
ask for a cloud of sweet, gentle
dreams and lullabies of hope
and love to form around their
children. They implore the good
night for gardens of reflection
that sing to the quiet moon, when
the world loses time and moves
into forever space and gives out
songs that were already written.
The night's light of opaque granite
only thieves pass through, their
bags full of sharpness work in
shadows because children see the
sun. The dark world, which always
leaks a little into light like a dripping
valve, the enamored sun with one
eye open shuts back in at dawn.

Little stars still fall from heavenly azure
amongst wisps of white
even with eyes too busy to see.

The Trombone Player

The baby played a trombone
on his Mother's bosom.
The music vibrating the
calm peaceful air.
Like the song he heard on the radio
from the womb.
With an old soul
from the mouth of hills and seas.

Toots blast out the other end too.

Little Suns

Look at how happiness spills from children's eyes.
Children are like little suns—
they wade into sepia beach water in late summer,
like alligators low in wetland.

Their bodies joyful, doing the simplest things.
Laughs brim on their faces when the slightest thing
is said that could contain at depth joy.
Their arms little forks on the water, splashing
the fish, their laughter rippling the sunset.

How could this delightful earth not be fun?
they say silently in a spread of smiling eyes.
Like the animals, they are not anything
other than what they are. In turn,
their presence is as full as the moon
made of sweet wildflowers.

The Children's Questions

Without a body how will the innocent
child, hurt and suffering, find her family?
Who are we?

Their questions bigger than the world.

A Day, an Adventure

A day with sticks children pick out like candy.
The sheep dogs lap at heels, ears flopping
like wings, noses turned to the bright,
laughing with open mouths, out for hours.

When they do come in, they draw a world
with stars for eyes, a heart-shaped sun,
and life with an upturned mouth.
They hand out imagination in bundles,
gifts from their play store. An invention
just fit for flicking toy pieces
across the world, a world full of beautiful
nonsense that makes perfect sense.

All the moments held together with charm
like a river's never-ending thread,
you forget what day it is—
why wouldn't we live in the world
of utter enchantment?

The Maze Garden

The friends ran through the garden of sculpted shrubs
like mice in a maze, dead ended at benches
to reflect on where you went wrong.
They helped a child, abashedly lost, calling out
in chorus mother, mother, to find only whispers
in echo. Hung their chins from a limb of a strangely
pruned pine laughing about where to go on a
pretend map. Threw their copper wishes into an
old fountain where live cherubs and wide-mouthed
bass, their coins thrown into eternity with other timeless
things like songs and memories and watching stars.
Changing tragic endings into arches, with their
smiling eyes, they kissed the world, saying, thank you,
I am alive.

The Child's Heart

Child bowed to the ground
in earnest
to pick the perfect acorn.
The key to unlock
the magical world.
Everybody inhabits,
nobody knows.

Barbed-Wire Spools

Spools of barbed wire furled in rust,
ready to trip children following a red admiral
off an enchanted path, and send them to bed
with paroxysms. With their large eyes growing
in a dream, their feet walking up the stairs
to a cloud. Saved by hoarders, who forgot
time uses things too. Like the gray squirrel
diligently collecting acorns and morsels for
long winter months. And bees busily visiting
the last flower to find nectar before a frost,
building up a pantry and cellar full of bags
of goods, saved for when we need it, like a
good story or a poem that shares in the world—
to hold in your pocket every wonderful thing
in life.

The Most Human Among Us

I once heard children were
the most human among us.
I do what I can to pay attention
to joy, when the world holds
my attention away, life slips out
my soles, when I'm not looking.
There are the wholesome among us,
the trees quietly doing their thing,
the moss crawling peaceably and
powerfully, the wind not growing
more softly or more loudly
than it must in one spot in time.
The rock is sitting, almost in prayer
and meditation. They make humans
look busy with trifle and tribulation.
What if those beings, doing their thing
in their soft, textured and unique spirit
without fanfare or eyes on gratitude,
are showing us, like all the children,
how to live?

On the North Shore

The great lake rocks to the moon and curls
its fingers frothy white, clenching its power
into a heart. I follow suit, along with humanity,
and lose my body to gain my innocence back,
licking melted chocolate off a banana boat,
while sitting around a campfire, knowing
this is all you need. To embody the purpose
of childhood, skipping rocks along the
snowcapped precipices of tiny moving
mountains, into a moment that lasts forever,
on the great lake lapping its tongue like a dog
and brandishing its power for queens to look
like ants. The rocks damp and dark in perennial
life and atrophy, falling to the sea bed to change
into God's next decision.

This Old World

Still life, in burgundy, rust, and stark white,
resting in reflection.
Drawing more purity and blood than exists within.
Pink, orange ribbons wrapping the shallow
azure roof,
clouds outlined in golden light more glorious
than a multitude of cathedral domes.

This old world is still more beautiful
than I can imagine,
still more than my eyes can let in,
always budding with youth,
always full of wisdom.
The buckthorn prickles us along the way,
crept invasively in—
I wonder how long before the beauty
in its colors
takes over its spot again.

Acknowledgments

A special thanks to Natalie. And thanks to the following journals and anthology where some of these poems, often in earlier versions, originally appeared:

Alchemy and Miracles Anthology: "Hungry Wind, Early Morning, Cold Spell," "A Thousand Setting Suns"

Martin Lake Journal: "The Ghost Herds," "In Sickness"

Minnesota Voices: "Scribbles of a Child," "Flight of the Peacock"

Poems of Hope and Reassurance: "Fields of Quiet," "Blossoms by the Bed," "Little Suns"

About the Author

Julie Adrian is a writer and educator living on a small farm in Minnesota with her family and dogs. Her work has recently appeared in Time of Singing, Talking Stick, the Alchemy and Miracles Anthology, and other journals. This is her first collection.

As a first grader, Julie began keeping a journal. After college, she set out to master the craft of writing, working with journalists, editors, and writers in Washington, DC. She loves writing about what is there and not seen through imagery in nature and everyday life.

www.ingramcontent.com/pod-product-compliance
Lightning Source LLC
Chambersburg PA
CBHW022128160426
43197CB00009B/1190